This journal belongs to:

Name: NASHAUN GRAHAM

Phone:

Email:

Instagram: @Lg-Nails London

Facebook: Lg nails London

A GUIDED JOURNAL *for* 2019

MAXINE HOLLY JONES

BALBOA PRESS
A DIVISION OF HAY HOUSE

Balboa Press books may be ordered through booksellers or by contacting:

Balboa Press
A Division of Hay House
1663 Liberty Drive
Bloomington, IN 47403
www.balboapress.co.uk
1 (877) 407-4847

Print information available on the last page.

ISBN: 978-1-9822-8018-5 (sc)
ISBN: 978-1-9822-8017-8 (e)

Balboa Press rev. date: 08/09/2018

try to check in once every day and when a negative thought enters your mind, imagine a wrestling ring and a positive thought knocking out the negative one! Try to put a positive spin on things, or simply redirect your thinking in a more positive direction.

Start by intentionally choosing positivity; with time your brain will rewire to sub-consciously choose positivity, and it will start to happen without you having to think about it.

Lunar chart

I have noted the new moon and full moon lunar days in the daily journal because these days carry energy that we can harness to strengthen our manifestations or clear away negativity.

New moons welcome new beginnings, new adventures and positive changes. This is a good time to decide what you want to create and set intentions for the month ahead. The journal plots new moon days as wish days to encourage you to dream and start planning what you want. The energy generated by everyone using the journal wishing altogether on this day multiplies the power and attracts greater positivity in our lives.

Full moons provide an opportunity to let go and release old or negative patterns that no longer serve you. The conclusive energy marks the end of a cycle and is a good time to celebrate good things that have happened and move forward with new positive intentions.

Goal setting – dream big!

Before we start the manifesting process, we need to look at the big picture and then focus in on specific areas.

On the next page there is space to write down twenty life goals. Dream big and imagine what you would like to achieve or attract into your life, as if failure is not an option. Include at least one goal for each of the following areas of your life; your health, family and relationships, career, material things, spirituality, personal growth and how you relax and enjoy life. Write down twenty goals, be daring and bold, and if you think of more, continue your list and keep writing in the notes section at the back of this book.

Refer back to this list of goals to help keep your mind focused on what is important to you throughout the year. Each day think about small steps you can take to achieve these bigger goals and fill in this next section as you go, no matter how ambitious, anything is possible!

Thursday 3rd January 2019

My manifesting mantra for today:

AM
9
10
11
12
1
2
3
4
5
PM

What is my passion in life, or what things make me happy?

What about this makes me feel happiness?

How can I dedicate time to these pursuits of happiness?

My thoughts and feelings today:

Friday 4th January 2019

My manifesting mantra for today:

AM

9

10

11

12

1

2

3

4

5

PM

How has my energy vibration flowed this week?

What has worked well, or not worked well this week?

How can I take a small step towards my best case scenario for this year?

My thoughts and feelings today:

Monday 7th January 2019

My manifesting mantra for today:

AM
9
10
11
12
1
2
3
4
5
PM

A small step I will take this week towards one of my life goals:

My priorities this week:

Remember and note down a moment when you felt loved:

My thoughts and feelings today:

Tuesday 8th January 2019

My manifesting mantra for today:

AM
9
10
11
12
1
2
3
4
5
PM

Who is important to me?

I appreciate this person in my life because:

Something nice I can do for them this week:

My thoughts and feelings today:

Wednesday 9th January 2019

My manifesting mantra for today:

AM
9
10
11
12
1
2
3
4
5
PM

Choose a love/family/friendship relationship in your life:

What kind of person I am like in this relationship?

How can I improve my actions to make the relationship better?

My thoughts and feelings today:

Thursday 10th January 2019

My manifesting mantra for today:

AM
9
10
11
12
1
2
3
4
5
PM

Start practising random acts of kindness and record them here:

How have other people impacted your life today?

How did their actions make you feel and what was your response?

My thoughts and feelings today:

"You cannot do a kindness too soon, for you never know how soon it will be too late" - Ralph Waldo Emerson

Friday 11th January 2019

My manifesting mantra for today:

AM
9
10
11
12
1
2
3
4
5
PM

Who have you enjoyed being around recently, and why?

Can you think of any non-physical gifts you've received recently - someone's time, attention, support?

What simple pleasures did you enjoy, or can you enjoy, today?

My thoughts and feelings today:

Saturday 12th January 2019

My manifesting mantra for today:

AM
9
10
11
12
1
2
3
4
5
PM

What have I given to the people in my life today?

What have I received from the people in my life today?

Does the give and take flow in my relationships feel equal?

My thoughts and feelings today:

Sunday 13th January 2019

My manifesting mantra for today:

AM
9
10
11
12
1
2
3
4
5
PM

How have I made progress towards my life goals this week?

I am grateful for:
1.
2.
3.

My thoughts and feelings today:

"The only time you fail is when you fall down and stay down"
- Stephen Richards

Monday 14th January 2019

My manifesting mantra for today:

AM
9
10
11
12
1
2
3
4
5
PM

My daily work / job / career is:

What do I enjoy about it?

How can I use it to make progress in my life?

My thoughts and feelings today:

Tuesday 15th January 2019

My manifesting mantra for today:

AM
9
10
11
12
1
2
3
4
5
PM

My daily work goal to achieve this week:

What can I do today to achieve my daily work goal?

Reward if/when my daily work goal is achieved:

My thoughts and feelings today:

Wednesday 16th January 2019

My manifesting mantra for today:

AM
9
10
11
12
1
2
3
4
5
PM

Practise being present and improving your focus. When we are truly in the moment, we are productive and time flies by. This is the ideal mind set for work! Each moment we experience is all we have; the past is gone, the future yet to come. Making the most of this moment, whether it be at work, with your family or a daily chore, is the key to making the most of your life.

My thoughts and feelings today:

Thursday 17th January 2019

My manifesting mantra for today:

AM

9

10

11

12

1

2

3

4

5

PM

In terms of my daily work, where do I see myself in two years?

If anything was possible where would I like to see myself in two years?

What can I do now to meet my expectations for the future?

My thoughts and feelings today:

Friday 18th January 2019

My manifesting mantra for today:

AM
9
10
11
12
1
2
3
4
5
PM

What went well this week?

What didn't go so well?

What have I learnt from those experiences?

My thoughts and feelings today:

Saturday 19th January 2019

My manifesting mantra for today:

AM
9
10
11
12
1
2
3
4
5
PM

How have I used my free time lately?

Has that helped me to feel inspired, vibrant, healthy and fulfilled?

What changes could I make to feel more fulfilled?

My thoughts and feelings today:

Sunday 20th January 2019

My manifesting mantra for today:

AM
9
10
11
12
1
2
3
4
5
PM

Have I made progress towards or achieved my daily work goal?

If so, how? If not, why?

What's improved about my life from this time last year?

My thoughts and feelings today:

Monday 21st January 2019

My manifesting mantra for today:

AM

9

10

11

12

1

2

3

4

5

PM

Take a moment today to release any negative tension you have felt recently. Holding negative thoughts within makes you suffer, so take positive action. Change the situation, or find a way to accept and let it go. Note down any thoughts that come to mind.

My thoughts and feelings today:

Tuesday 22nd January 2019

My manifesting mantra for today:

AM
9
10
11
12
1
2
3
4
5
PM

My goal for the week ahead:

That will help me achieve my life goal of:

My priorities this week:

My thoughts and feelings today:

Wednesday 23rd January 2019

My manifesting mantra for today:

AM
9
10
11
12
1
2
3
4
5
PM

Did I follow my intuition today and what did it tell me?

Practise connecting to your intuition: clear your mind, take three deep breaths, ask a question and trust the first thought that comes into your head. Note down the question and answer here:

Question:

Answer:

My thoughts and feelings today:

Thursday 24th January 2019

My manifesting mantra for today:

AM
9
10
11
12
1
2
3
4
5
PM

Practise the art of manifesting. Choose something small, sit back and observe how the Universe picks up on it. Little signs will appear around you. A song on the radio, something you see...

Write down your manifesting thought:

Note down the signs you receive:

My thoughts and feelings today:

Friday 25th January 2019

My manifesting mantra for today:

AM
9
10
11
12
1
2
3
4
5
PM

What have I learnt so far this week?

If you did not receive what you wanted this week, can you identify something you received that is worth having?

Something I will do to invest in my happiness and wellbeing this weekend:

My thoughts and feelings today:

Saturday 26th January 2019

My manifesting mantra for today:

AM

9

10

11

12

1

2

3

4

5

PM

What's the best thing that happened this month?

How can I create similar experiences?

If I could have anything, what would I ask the universe for?

My thoughts and feelings today:

"Optimism is a happiness magnet. If you stay positive, good things and good people will be drawn to you" - *Mary Lou Retton*

Sunday 27th January 2019

My manifesting mantra for today:

AM

9

10

11

12

1

2

3

4

5

PM

Have I made progress towards or achieved my weekly goal?

If so, how? If not, why?

Am I proud of who I am, how I behave and what I offer to this world?

My thoughts and feelings today:

Monday 28th January 2019

My manifesting mantra for today:

AM

9

10

11

12

1

2

3

4

5

PM

A small step I will take this week towards one of my life goals:

My priorities this week:

Have you experienced any blessings in disguise lately - something that didn't turn out as you'd hoped, yet turned out for the best?

My thoughts and feelings today:

Tuesday 29th January 2019

My manifesting mantra for today:

AM
9
10
11
12
1
2
3
4
5
PM

Three things I like about myself:
1.
2.
3.

Three things I would like to improve about myself:
1.
2.
3.

My thoughts and feelings today:

Wednesday 30th January 2019

My manifesting mantra for today:

AM
9
10
11
12
1
2
3
4
5
PM

How is my emotional vibration today?

How has my emotional vibration fluctuated this month?

How can I improve my emotional vibration day to day?

My thoughts and feelings today:

Thursday 31st January 2019

My manifesting mantra for today:

AM
9
10
11
12
1
2
3
4
5
PM

What are my top achievements this month?

What negative emotions did I experience this month?

Am I happy with the way I spent my time this month?

My thoughts and feelings today:

Friday 1st February 2019

My manifesting mantra for today:

AM
9
10
11
12
1
2
3
4
5
PM

My goal for February:

Reward if achieved:

Something I will do this weekend, just for me, to make me happy:

My thoughts and feelings today:

Saturday 2nd February 2019

My manifesting mantra for today:

AM

9

10

11

12

1

2

3

4

5

PM

Visualise your ideal life and describe here:

How can you bring your ideal life into your everyday life:

What small step can you take now to bring your ideal life into reality:

My thoughts and feelings today:

Sunday 3rd February 2019

My manifesting mantra for today:

AM
9
10
11
12
1
2
3
4
5
PM

Three things I am grateful for:
1.
2.
3.

What did I learn from this week?

My thoughts and feelings today:

Wednesday 6th February 2019

My manifesting mantra for today:

AM
9
10
11
12
1
2
3
4
5
PM

How often have you completed your morning ritual created last month?

Today is a reminder about your morning ritual and a chance to change it. Does it work for you? What might work better?

My thoughts and feelings today:

Thursday 7th February 2019

My manifesting mantra for today:

AM
9
10
11
12
1
2
3
4
5
PM

Who's needs do I consider day to day?

How well do I prioritise my needs against the needs of others?

Am I dedicating enough time to the pursuit of my happiness?

My thoughts and feelings today:

Friday 8th February 2019

My manifesting mantra for today:

AM

9

10

11

12

1

2

3

4

5

PM

How has my energy vibration flowed this week?

What has worked well or not worked well this week?

How can I take a small step towards my best case scenario for this year?

My thoughts and feelings today:

Saturday 9th February 2019

My manifesting mantra for today:

AM
9
10
11
12
1
2
3
4
5
PM

What about today will add to my quality of life?

Am I enjoying my life's journey so far?

I am lucky because:

My thoughts and feelings today:

"Honour your desire for a new life. Say yes to the small inklings of interest and curiosity that present themselves each day"
- Lynn Robinson

Tuesday 12th February 2019

My manifesting mantra for today:

AM
9
10
11
12
1
2
3
4
5
PM

Who is important to me?

I appreciate this person in my life because:

Something nice I can do for them this week:

My thoughts and feelings today:

Wednesday 13th February 2019

My manifesting mantra for today:

AM

9

10

11

12

1

2

3

4

5

PM

Choose a love/family/friendship relationship in your life:

What kind of person am I like in this relationship?

How can I improve my actions to make the relationship better?

My thoughts and feelings today:

Thursday 14th February 2019

My manifesting mantra for today:
love others, show tokens of appreciation

AM
9
10
11
12
1
2
3
4
5
PM

My random acts of kindness:

How have other people impacted your life today?
they make me want to show them

How did their actions make you feel and what was your response?

My thoughts and feelings today:

My manifesting mantra for today:

AM
9
10
11
12
1
2
3
4
5
PM

What did I learn so far this week?

Did I allow things to flow this week without trying to control the outcome?

Something I can do this weekend just for me:

My thoughts and feelings today:

Saturday 16th February 2019

My manifesting mantra for today:

AM

9

10

11

12

1

2

3

4

5

PM

Which relationship in my life needs more of my attention and love right now?

Is there any relationship in my life that is toxic or any person who drains my sense of self?

Recognise the difference between the two relationships above and dedicate your time to those who deserve it.

My thoughts and feelings today:

Sunday 17th February 2019

My manifesting mantra for today:

AM
9
10
11
12
1
2
3
4
5
PM

How have I made progress towards my life goals this week?

My gratitude list this week:
1.
2.
3.

My thoughts and feelings today:

Friday 22nd February 2019

My manifesting mantra for today:

AM
9
10
11
12
1
2
3
4
5
PM

What have I learnt so far this week?

Is there anything I intended to achieve that did not happen? Why?

What I am looking forward to this weekend:

My thoughts and feelings today:

Saturday 23rd February 2019

My manifesting mantra for today:

AM
9
10
11
12
1
2
3
4
5
PM

How do I take time out from work to relax?

Do I have a good work life balance?

What can I do to improve my work life balance?

My thoughts and feelings today:

"I always do a mental audit at the end of the week to make sure I'm balancing time between my career and my personal life"
- Jill Wagner

Sunday 24th February 2019

My manifesting mantra for today:

AM

9

10

11

12

1

2

3

4

5

PM

Have I made progress towards or achieved my daily work goal?

If so, how? If not, why?

Something I have enjoyed about my daily work recently:

My thoughts and feelings today:

Monday 25th February 2019

My manifesting mantra for today:

AM
9
10
11
12
1
2
3
4
5
PM

My goal for the week ahead:

That will help me achieve my life goal of:

My priorities this week:

My thoughts and feelings today:

Tuesday 26th February 2019

My manifesting mantra for today:

AM
9
10
11
12
1
2
3
4
5
PM

How has this month added to the quality of my life?

Am I enjoying the journey? How can I make it better?

Remember and note down a moment when you felt connected to nature / the universe / life's source:

My thoughts and feelings today:

"Travelers, we are not human beings on a spiritual journey, we are Spiritual beings on a human journey" - Native American saying

Wednesday 27th February 2019

My manifesting mantra for today:

AM
9
10
11
12
1
2
3
4
5
PM

Do I feel a connection to my gut instinct? Do I listen to it?

Practise connecting to your intuition: clear your mind, take three deep breaths, ask a question and trust the first thought that comes into your head. Note down the question and answer here:

Question:

Answer:

My thoughts and feelings today:

Thursday 28st February 2019

My manifesting mantra for today:

AM
9
10
11
12
1
2
3
4
5
PM

What were my happiest moments in the past month?

What obstacles or fears did I experience this month?

How do I feel about my progress this month?

My thoughts and feelings today:

Friday 1st March 2019

My manifesting mantra for today:

AM
9
10
11
12
1
2
3
4
5
PM

My goal for March:

Reward if/when achieved:

What is the best possible outcome at the end of this month?

My thoughts and feelings today:

Saturday 2nd March 2019

My manifesting mantra for today:

AM
9
10
11
12
1
2
3
4
5
PM

How is my emotional vibration today?

How has my emotional vibration fluctuated this week?

How can I improve my emotional vibration day to day?

My thoughts and feelings today:

Sunday 3rd March 2019

My manifesting mantra for today:

AM
9
10
11
12
1
2
3
4
5
PM

Have I made progress towards or achieved my weekly goal?

If so, how? If not, why?

Things I am grateful for:

My thoughts and feelings today:

Wednesday 6th March 2019

My manifesting mantra for today:

AM
9
10
11
12
1
2
3
4
5
PM

Make a wish – it's a new moon today:

Create an evening ritual to help you unwind and de-stress. Think of something you can do every night before you go to sleep to rebalance your energy vibration:

My thoughts and feelings today:

Thursday 7th March 2019

My manifesting mantra for today:

AM

9

10

11

12

1

2

3

4

5

PM

What is my definition of a happy life:

Do I feel that I have a happy life?

Practical things I can do to choose happiness:

My thoughts and feelings today:

Friday 8th March 2019

My manifesting mantra for today:

AM

9

10

11

12

1

2

3

4

5

PM

How has my energy vibration flowed this week?

What has worked well or not worked well this week?

How can I take a small step towards my best case scenario for this year?

My thoughts and feelings today:

Saturday 9th March 2019

My manifesting mantra for today:

AM

9

10

11

12

1

2

3

4

5

PM

What have I been day dreaming about lately?

Have I spent time focusing my thoughts on positivity and what I want to happen?

Has the Universe given me any signs that it is listening?

My thoughts and feelings today:

Thursday 14th March 2019

My manifesting mantra for today:

AM
9
10
11
12
1
2
3
4
5
PM

My random acts of kindness:

How have other people impacted your life lately?

How did their actions make you feel and what was your response?

My thoughts and feelings today:

Friday 15th March 2019

My manifesting mantra for today:

AM
9
10
11
12
1
2
3
4
5
PM

What did I learn so far this week?

What non-physical gifts have you received recently - someone's time, attention, support?

Who have you enjoyed being around recently, and why?

My thoughts and feelings today:

Saturday 16th March 2019

My manifesting mantra for today:

AM

9

10

11

12

1

2

3

4

5

PM

What have I given to the people in my life this week?

What have I received from the people in my life this week?

Does the give and take flow in my relationships feel equal?

My thoughts and feelings today:

Sunday 17th March 2019

My manifesting mantra for today:

AM
9
10
11
12
1
2
3
4
5
PM

How have I made progress towards my life goals this week?

Three things I am grateful for:
1.
2.
3.

My thoughts and feelings today:

"The only place your dream becomes impossible is in your own thinking"
- Robert H Schuller

Monday 18th March 2019

My manifesting mantra for today:

AM
9
10
11
12
1
2
3
4
5
PM

My daily work goal to achieve this week:

What can I do today to achieve my daily work goal?

Reward if/when my daily work goal is achieved:

My thoughts and feelings today:

Tuesday 19th March 2019

My manifesting mantra for today:

AM

9

10

11

12

1

2

3

4

5

PM

Am I feeling professionally fulfilled / satisfied with my daily work?

What would I most like to learn in the next twelve months?

What are my strengths and achievements in the past year that I can celebrate?

My thoughts and feelings today:

Wednesday 20th March 2019

My manifesting mantra for today:

AM
9
10
11
12
1
2
3
4
5
PM

I was once told that when you meditate you become an observer of the mind; you observe the thoughts and emotions of your brain as if you are an external entity. Take a step back and observe how your emotions ebb and flow or flare up throughout each day. When you feel emotions taking over, stop and smile. Become aware of the immediate physiological response in your body and take back control of your mind. Choose happiness.

My thoughts and feelings today:

"The art of life lies in a constant readjustment to our surroundings"
- Okakura Kakuzo

Thursday 21st March 2019

My manifesting mantra for today:

AM

9

10

11

12

1

2

3

4

5

PM

Imagine the full moon as the end of a phase and celebrate all of the wonderful things that have happened during this time, however small. Take time to go outside and admire its beauty. Mention everything that you are grateful for and then set your intentions for what you would like the Universe to bring to your life for the month to come. Say it out loud and let the Universe take care of it. Record your intentions below:

My thoughts and feelings today:

Friday 22nd March 2019

My manifesting mantra for today:

AM

9

10

11

12

1

2

3

4

5

PM

How has my energy vibration flowed this week?

What has worked well, or not worked well this week?

How can I take a small step towards my best case scenario for this year?

My thoughts and feelings today:

Saturday 23rd March 2019

My manifesting mantra for today:

AM
9
10
11
12
1
2
3
4
5
PM

How have I been using my free time lately?

Has that helped me to feel inspired, vibrant, healthy and fulfilled?

What changes could I make to feel more fulfilled?

My thoughts and feelings today:

Sunday 24th March 2019

My manifesting mantra for today:

AM
9
10
11
12
1
2
3
4
5
PM

Have I made progress towards or achieved my daily work goal?

If so, how? If not, why?

My reflections from this week are:

My thoughts and feelings today:

Monday 25th March 2019

My manifesting mantra for today:

AM

9

10

11

12

1

2

3

4

5

PM

My goal for the week ahead:

That will help me achieve my life goal of:

My priorities this week:

My thoughts and feelings today:

My manifesting mantra for today:

AM
9
10
11
12
1
2
3
4
5
PM

Practise the art of manifesting. Choose something small, sit back and observe how the Universe picks up on it. Little signs will appear around you. A song on the radio, something you see...

Write down your manifesting thought:

Note down the signs you receive:

My thoughts and feelings today:

Wednesday 27th March 2019

My manifesting mantra for today:

AM
9
10
11
12
1
2
3
4
5
PM

Something beautiful you have seen in this world recently:

Practise connecting to your intuition: clear your mind, take three deep breaths, ask a question and trust the first thought that comes into your head. Note down the question and answer here:

Question:

Answer:

My thoughts and feelings today:

Thursday 28th March 2019

My manifesting mantra for today:

AM

9

10

11

12

1

2

3

4

5

PM

My current habits for eating, drinking and exercising:

Are my current habits working for me or against me?

How can I change my habits to work for me?

My thoughts and feelings today:

Friday 29th March 2019

My manifesting mantra for today:

AM
9
10
11
12
1
2
3
4
5
PM

What feelings dominated my experience of life this month?

What feelings do I want to experience in the month to come?

Am I proud of who I am, how I behave and what I offer to this world?

My thoughts and feelings today:

Saturday 30th March 2019

My manifesting mantra for today:

AM
9
10
11
12
1
2
3
4
5
PM

What positive choices have you made in the past month?

What are you looking forward to next month?

Am I living a life that is meaningful to me?

My thoughts and feelings today:

"The next time you feel slightly uncomfortable with the pressure in your life, remember no pressure, no diamonds. Pressure is part of success"
- Eric Thomas

Sunday 31st March 2019

My manifesting mantra for today:

AM
9
10
11
12
1
2
3
4
5
PM

What were my happiest moments in the past month?

What obstacles or fears did I experience this month?

How do I feel about my progress this month?

My thoughts and feelings today:

My manifesting mantra for today:

AM
9
10
11
12
1
2
3
4
5
PM

My goal for April:

Reward if/when achieved:

My priorities this week:

My thoughts and feelings today:

Tuesday 2nd April 2019

My manifesting mantra for today:

AM
9
10
11
12
1
2
3
4
5
PM

A small step I will take this week towards one of my life goals:

What am I happy about in my life right now?

What would I like to change about my life right now?

My thoughts and feelings today:

"Every word you speak is a prayer, or meditation of reinforcement which creates permanence" - Bryant McGill

Wednesday 3rd April 2019

My manifesting mantra for today:

AM

9

10

11

12

1

2

3

4

5

PM

Something I will do this week, just for me, to make me happy:

If you had an extra hour in the day, what would you do with it?

When was the last time you felt most excited or alive?

My thoughts and feelings today:

Thursday 4th April 2019

My manifesting mantra for today:

AM
9
10
11
12
1
2
3
4
5
PM

What small changes could you make to improve your day?

What is something that always makes you smile?

Am I dedicating enough time to the pursuit of my happiness?

My thoughts and feelings today:

Friday 5th April 2019

My manifesting mantra for today:

AM
9
10
11
12
1
2
3
4
5
PM

Make a wish – it's a new moon today:

How has my energy vibration flowed this week?

How can I take a small step towards my best case scenario for this year?

My thoughts and feelings today:

Saturday 6th April 2019

My manifesting mantra for today:

AM
9
10
11
12
1
2
3
4
5
PM

What small things can I do to live my life to the fullest, today?

Am I enjoying my life's journey so far?

I am lucky because:

My thoughts and feelings today:

My manifesting mantra for today:

AM
9
10
11
12
1
2
3
4
5
PM

How did I make myself feel good this week?

How have I made progress towards my life goals this week?

What can I do to make next week better than this one?

My thoughts and feelings today:

Monday 8th April 2019

My manifesting mantra for today:

AM
9
10
11
12
1
2
3
4
5
PM

A small step I will take this week towards one of my life goals:

My priorities this week:

Remember and note down a moment when you felt loved:

My thoughts and feelings today:

Tuesday 9th April 2019

My manifesting mantra for today:

AM
9
10
11
12
1
2
3
4
5
PM

Who is important to me?

I appreciate this person in my life because:

Something nice I can do for them this week:

My thoughts and feelings today:

Wednesday 10th April 2019

My manifesting mantra for today:

AM

9

10

11

12

1

2

3

4

5

PM

Choose a love/family/friendship relationship in your life:

What kind of person am I like in this relationship?

How can I improve my actions to make the relationship better?

My thoughts and feelings today:

Thursday 11th April 2019

My manifesting mantra for today:

AM
9
10
11
12
1
2
3
4
5
PM

My random acts of kindness:

How have other people impacted your life lately?

How did their actions make you feel and what was your response?

My thoughts and feelings today:

Friday 12th April 2019

My manifesting mantra for today:

AM

9

10

11

12

1

2

3

4

5

PM

What was my soul's lesson this week?

Who are the five people I spend the most time with?

Are these people enabling me or holding me back?

My thoughts and feelings today:

Wednesday 17th April 2019

My manifesting mantra for today:

AM

9

10

11

12

1

2

3

4

5

PM

What was I doing this time a year ago? How was I feeling?

Would I be happy with what I am doing now?

What do I want to be doing a year from now?

My thoughts and feelings today:

Thursday 18th April 2019

My manifesting mantra for today:

AM
9
10
11
12
1
2
3
4
5
PM

What are my ambitions?

Am I moving in the right direction towards realising my ambitions?

What do I want to learn next?

My thoughts and feelings today:

Friday 19th April 2019

My manifesting mantra for today:

AM
9
10
11
12
1
2
3
4
5
PM

Spend five minutes today thinking about all the positive things in your life and write them below. Thank the Universe for all you have. Look in the mirror and say nice things to yourself! During a full moon your positive thoughts will be energised and multiplied.

My thoughts and feelings today:

Saturday 20th April 2019

My manifesting mantra for today:

AM
9
10
11
12
1
2
3
4
5
PM

What went well this week?

What didn't go so well?

What have I learnt from those experiences?

My thoughts and feelings today:

"When we are no longer able to change a situation, we are challenged to change ourselves" - Viktor Frankl

Sunday 21st April 2019

My manifesting mantra for today:

AM
9
10
11
12
1
2
3
4
5
PM

Have I made progress towards or achieved my daily work goal?

If so, how? If not, why?

My favourite song at the moment and how it makes me feel:

My thoughts and feelings today:

Monday 22nd April 2019

My manifesting mantra for today:

AM
9
10
11
12
1
2
3
4
5
PM

My goal for the week ahead:

That will help me achieve my life goal of:

My priorities this week:

My thoughts and feelings today:

Tuesday 23rd April 2019

My manifesting mantra for today:

AM
9
10
11
12
1
2
3
4
5
PM

What one thing would bring me more satisfaction in my life?

What have I done in the past month to attain it?

What will I do in the next month to attain it?

My thoughts and feelings today:

Wednesday 24th April 2019

My manifesting mantra for today:

AM
9
10
11
12
1
2
3
4
5
PM

How would I describe myself?

What qualities do I want to embody?

Something I like about my character and personality:

My thoughts and feelings today:

My manifesting mantra for today:

AM
9
10
11
12
1
2
3
4
5
PM

What is my bucket list? Three things I want to do before I die:

1.
2.
3.

How would I spend the next day if it were my last:

My thoughts and feelings today:

"Whatever you focus on, think about, read about and talk about intensely, you're going to attract into your life"
- Jack Canfield

Friday 26th April 2019

My manifesting mantra for today:

AM

9

10

11

12

1

2

3

4

5

PM

How has today contributed to the grand scheme of my life?

How can I find ways to appreciate each day I am blessed to have?

How can I take a small step towards my best case scenario for this year?

My thoughts and feelings today:

Saturday 27th April 2019

My manifesting mantra for today:

AM
9
10
11
12
1
2
3
4
5
PM

What or whom have I positively contributed to today?

Has that helped me to feel inspired, vibrant, healthy and fulfilled?

Something small can I start doing to be of service to the world?

My thoughts and feelings today:

Sunday 28th April 2019

My manifesting mantra for today:

AM
9
10
11
12
1
2
3
4
5
PM

Have I made progress towards or achieved my goal this week?

If so, how? If not, why?

I am grateful for:

My thoughts and feelings today:

Monday 29th April 2019

My manifesting mantra for today:

AM
9
10
11
12
1
2
3
4
5
PM

What were my happiest moments in the past month?

What negative emotions did I experience this month?

How do I feel about my personal progress this month?

My thoughts and feelings today:

Tuesday 30th April 2019

My manifesting mantra for today:

AM

9

10

11

12

1

2

3

4

5

PM

What are my top achievements this month?

Am I happy with how I used my time this month?

What was my soul's lesson this month?

My thoughts and feelings today:

Wednesday 1st May 2019

My manifesting mantra for today:

AM
9
10
11
12
1
2
3
4
5
PM

My goal for May:

Reward if/when achieved:

What is the best possible situation at the end of this month?

My thoughts and feelings today:

Thursday 2nd May 2019

My manifesting mantra for today:

AM

9

10

11

12

1

2

3

4

5

PM

Am I living the life I chose for myself – or someone else's ideal?

Am I spending my time on what I value most?

Is there anything I can change day to day to be happier?

My thoughts and feelings today:

My manifesting mantra for today:

AM
9
10
11
12
1
2
3
4
5
PM

How has my energy vibration flowed this week?

What has worked well or not worked well this week?

How can I take a small step towards my best case scenario for this year? Has it changed?

My thoughts and feelings today:

Saturday 4th May 2019

My manifesting mantra for today:

AM
9
10
11
12
1
2
3
4
5
PM

Make a wish – it's a new moon today:

What things in my life have made me feel happy lately?

How can I dedicate more of my time to these pursuits?

My thoughts and feelings today:

"Ask for what you want, and be prepared to get it" - Maya Angelou

Sunday 5th May 2019

My manifesting mantra for today:

AM

9

10

11

12

1

2

3

4

5

PM

Have I had more ups than downs lately?

How have I made progress towards my life goals this week?

What can I do to make next week better than this one?

My thoughts and feelings today:

Monday 6th May 2019

My manifesting mantra for today:

AM
9
10
11
12
1
2
3
4
5
PM

A small step I will take this week towards one of my life goals:

My priorities this week:

Who made a positive difference in my life recently?

My thoughts and feelings today:

Tuesday 7th May 2019

My manifesting mantra for today:

AM
9
10
11
12
1
2
3
4
5
PM

Are my actions consistent with what I say?

What culture do I want to create with my family? Culture being the traditions, habits, practices and values you have.

Which relationships should I devote more time to?

My thoughts and feelings today:

Wednesday 8th May 2019

My manifesting mantra for today:

AM
9
10
11
12
1
2
3
4
5
PM

Choose a love/family/friendship relationship in your life:

What kind of person am I like in this relationship?

How can I improve my actions to make the relationship better?

My thoughts and feelings today:

Thursday 9th May 2019

My manifesting mantra for today:

AM
9
10
11
12
1
2
3
4
5
PM

My random acts of kindness:

How have other people impacted your life lately?

How did their actions make you feel and what was your response?

My thoughts and feelings today:

Friday 10th May 2019

My manifesting mantra for today:

AM
9
10
11
12
1
2
3
4
5
PM

What did I learn so far this week?

Something you have witnessed recently that reminded you that people are good:

What simple pleasures did you enjoy, or can you enjoy, today?

My thoughts and feelings today:

My manifesting mantra for today:

AM

9

10

11

12

1

2

3

4

5

PM

What qualities do I have that make me a good friend?

What could I improve on?

Do I make enough effort with my friends and do I feel valued in return?

My thoughts and feelings today:

Sunday 12th May 2019

My manifesting mantra for today:

AM
9
10
11
12
1
2
3
4
5
PM

How have I made progress towards my life goals this week?

My gratitude list this week:
1.
2.
3.

My thoughts and feelings today:

Monday 13th May 2019

My manifesting mantra for today:

AM
9
10
11
12
1
2
3
4
5
PM

My daily work goal to achieve this week:

What can I do today to achieve my daily work goal?

Reward if/when my daily work goal is achieved:

My thoughts and feelings today:

"Success will be within your reach only when you start reaching out for it" - Stephen Richards

Tuesday 14th May 2019

My manifesting mantra for today:

AM
9
10
11
12
1
2
3
4
5
PM

How would I describe myself; a saver or a spender?

How can I make changes to save or spend money more wisely?

Set a specific goal about saving or spending for next month:

My thoughts and feelings today:

Sunday 19th May 2019

My manifesting mantra for today:

AM

9

10

11

12

1

2

3

4

5

PM

Have I made progress towards or achieved my daily work goal?

If so, how? If not, why?

My reflections from this week are:

My thoughts and feelings today:

My manifesting mantra for today:

AM

9

10

11

12

1

2

3

4

5

PM

My goal for the week ahead:

That will help me achieve my life goal of:

My priorities this week:

My thoughts and feelings today:

Tuesday 21st May 2019

My manifesting mantra for today:

AM
9
10
11
12
1
2
3
4
5
PM

What have I been day dreaming about lately?

Have I spent time focusing my thoughts on positivity and what I want to happen?

Has the Universe given me any signs that it is listening?

My thoughts and feelings today:

Wednesday 22nd May 2019

My manifesting mantra for today:

AM
9
10
11
12
1
2
3
4
5
PM

Did I follow my intuition today and what did it tell me?

Practise connecting to your intuition: clear your mind, take three deep breaths, ask a question and trust the first thought that comes into your head. Note down the question and answer here:

Question:

Answer:

My thoughts and feelings today:

Thursday 23rd May 2019

My manifesting mantra for today:

AM
9
10
11
12
1
2
3
4
5
PM

Three things that I worry about:
1.
2.
3.

Create positive affirmations to reprogram how you think about these worries:
1.
2.
3.

My thoughts and feelings today:

"I've had a lot of worries in my life, most of which never happened"
- Mark Twain

Friday 24th May 2019

My manifesting mantra for today:

AM

9

10

11

12

1

2

3

4

5

PM

What have I learnt so far this week?

Did I allow things to flow this week without trying to control the outcome?

Do something to invest in your happiness and wellbeing this weekend:

My thoughts and feelings today:

Saturday 25th May 2019

My manifesting mantra for today:

AM
9
10
11
12
1
2
3
4
5
PM

Is my body healthy?

What do I do that contributes to my health?

What do I do that works against my health?

My thoughts and feelings for today:

Sunday 26th May 2019

My manifesting mantra for today:

AM
9
10
11
12
1
2
3
4
5
PM

Have I made progress towards or achieved my weekly goal?

If so, how? If not, why?

My gratitude list this week:

My thoughts and feelings today:

Monday 27th May 2019

My manifesting mantra for today:

AM
9
10
11
12
1
2
3
4
5
PM

My goal for the week ahead:

That will help me achieve my life goal of:

My priorities this week:

My thoughts and feelings today:

Tuesday 28th May 2019

My manifesting mantra for today:

AM
9
10
11
12
1
2
3
4
5
PM

What am I looking forward to this week:

Something that made me laugh recently:

Something enjoyable you experience every day that you've come to take for granted:

My thoughts and feelings today:

Wednesday 29th May 2019

My manifesting mantra for today:

AM
9
10
11
12
1
2
3
4
5
PM

Three words to describe my emotional vibration today?

How has my emotional vibration fluctuated over the past month?

How can I improve my emotional vibration day to day?

My thoughts and feelings today:

Thursday 30th May 2019

My manifesting mantra for today:

AM
9
10
11
12
1
2
3
4
5
PM

What happened in the past month that made me feel good?

What happened in the past month that made me feel negative?

Am I happy with the way I spent my time this month?

My thoughts and feelings today:

My manifesting mantra for today:

AM

9

10

11

12

1

2

3

4

5

PM

What's the best thing that happened in the past month?

How can I create similar experiences?

If I could have anything, what would I ask the Universe for?

My thoughts and feelings today:

"It's unlimited what the Universe can bring when you understand the great secret that thoughts become things" - Anonymous

Saturday 1st June 2019

My manifesting mantra for today:

AM
9
10
11
12
1
2
3
4
5
PM

My goal for June:

Reward if/when achieved:

How can I live my life to the fullest this month?

My thoughts and feelings today:

Sunday 2nd June 2019

My manifesting mantra for today:

AM

9

10

11

12

1

2

3

4

5

PM

Have I made progress towards or achieved my weekly goal?

If so, how? If not, why?

Things I am looking forward to this month:

My thoughts and feelings today:

Monday 3rd June 2019

My manifesting mantra for today:

AM

9

10

11

12

1

2

3

4

5

PM

Make a wish – it's a new moon today:

My priorities this week:

Something I will do this week, just for me, to make me happy:

My thoughts and feelings today:

Tuesday 4th June 2019

My manifesting mantra for today:

AM
9
10
11
12
1
2
3
4
5
PM

What am I happy about in my life right now?

What is my deepest desire, right now:

A small step I will take this week towards one of my life goals:

My thoughts and feelings today:

"Think the thought until you believe it,
and once you believe it, it is"
- Abraham Hicks

Wednesday 5th June 2019

My manifesting mantra for today:

AM
9
10
11
12
1
2
3
4
5
PM

How important is routine to me and why?

How can I improve my morning ritual?

How can I improve my evening ritual?

My thoughts and feelings today:

My manifesting mantra for today:

AM
9
10
11
12
1
2
3
4
5
PM

Something I can do today to enhance my quality of life:

Am I enjoying my life's journey so far?

What's the best thing that happened this week so far:

My thoughts and feelings today:

Sunday 9th June 2019

My manifesting mantra for today:

AM

9

10

11

12

1

2

3

4

5

PM

How did I make myself feel good this week?

How have I made progress towards my life goals this week?

What can I do to make next week better than this one?

My thoughts and feelings today:

My manifesting mantra for today:

AM
9
10
11
12
1
2
3
4
5
PM

A small step I will take this week towards one of my life goals:

My priorities this week:

Remember and note down a moment when you felt appreciated:

My thoughts and feelings today:

My manifesting mantra for today:

AM
9
10
11
12
1
2
3
4
5
PM

Do I feel unconditionally loved by someone?

Do I contribute unconditional love to anyone?

Have I forgiven myself and others for mistakes, unconditionally?

My thoughts and feelings today:

Wednesday 12th June 2019

My manifesting mantra for today:

AM
9
10
11
12
1
2
3
4
5
PM

Choose a love/family/friendship relationship in your life:

Would I want to be the other person in this relationship with me?

How can I improve my actions to make the relationship better?

My thoughts and feelings today:

Thursday 13th June 2019

My manifesting mantra for today:

AM
9
10
11
12
1
2
3
4
5
PM

My random acts of kindness:

How have other people impacted your life today?

How did their actions make you feel and what was your response?

My thoughts and feelings today:

Friday 14th June 2019

My manifesting mantra for today:

AM
9
10
11
12
1
2
3
4
5
PM

What did I learn so far this week?

Did I allow things to flow this week without trying to control the outcome?

Something I can do this weekend just for me:

My thoughts and feelings today:

"Virtually nothing is impossible in this world if you just put your mind to it and maintain a positive attitude" - Lou Holtz

Saturday 15th June 2019

My manifesting mantra for today:

AM
9
10
11
12
1
2
3
4
5
PM

What do I expect from the people closest to me?

Do I emulate the same qualities to my nearest and dearest?

Who do you need to get in touch with because its been too long?

My thoughts and feelings today:

Sunday 16th June 2019

My manifesting mantra for today:

AM
9
10
11
12
1
2
3
4
5
PM

How have I made progress towards my life goals this week?

Three things I am grateful for:
1.
2.
3.

My thoughts and feelings today:

Monday 17th June 2019

My manifesting mantra for today:

AM
9
10
11
12
1
2
3
4
5
PM

Another lunar cycle, another opportunity to start again. Is there an aspect of your life that you would like to wipe the slate clean for? Now is the time to do that. Forgive yourself, forgive others. Mentally close the door on whatever it is that is not bringing light and love into your life. Make space so that when something new and positive arrives, there is somewhere for it to stay and become a part of your life.

My thoughts and feelings today:

Tuesday 18th June 2019

My manifesting mantra for today:

AM
9
10
11
12
1
2
3
4
5
PM

My daily work goal to achieve this week:

What can I do today to achieve my daily work goal?

Reward if/when my daily work goal is achieved:

My thoughts and feelings today:

My manifesting mantra for today:

AM
9
10
11
12
1
2
3
4
5
PM

Do you live to work, or work to live?

What is your number one priority, right now?

Are you happy with the way things are right now?

My thoughts and feelings today:

Thursday 20th June 2019

My manifesting mantra for today:

AM

9

10

11

12

1

2

3

4

5

PM

How has today contributed to the grand scheme of my life?

How can I find ways to appreciate each day I am blessed to have?

Am I enjoying using this journal and why?

My thoughts and feelings today:

Friday 21st June 2019

My manifesting mantra for today:

AM
9
10
11
12
1
2
3
4
5
PM

How has my energy vibration flowed this week?

What has worked well or not worked well this week?

How can I take a small step towards my best case scenario for this year?

My thoughts and feelings today:

Saturday 22nd June 2019

My manifesting mantra for today:

AM
9
10
11
12
1
2
3
4
5
PM

How have I been using my free time this month?

Has that helped me to feel inspired, vibrant, healthy and fulfilled?

What changes could I make to feel more fulfilled in my life?

My thoughts and feelings today:

Sunday 23rd June 2019

My manifesting mantra for today:

AM
9
10
11
12
1
2
3
4
5
PM

Have I made progress towards or achieved my daily work goal?

If so, how? If not, why?

My reflections from this week are:

My thoughts and feelings today:

Monday 24th June 2019

My manifesting mantra for today:

AM
9
10
11
12
1
2
3
4
5
PM

My goal for the week ahead:

That will help me achieve my life goal of:

My priorities this week:

My thoughts and feelings today:

"When you are clear about what you want, the Universe will often find ways of giving it to you" - Maya Fiennes

Tuesday 25th June 2019

My manifesting mantra for today:

AM

9

10

11

12

1

2

3

4

5

PM

What was your biggest worry five years ago?

Do you still feel the same about it?

What advice would you give that younger version of yourself, in that situation?

My thoughts and feelings today:

Wednesday 26th June 2019

My manifesting mantra for today:

AM
9
10
11
12
1
2
3
4
5
PM

Look out for signs from the Universe and note them down here:

Practise connecting to your intuition: clear your mind, take three deep breaths, ask a question and trust the first thought that comes into your head. Note down the question and answer here:

Question:

Answer:

My thoughts and feelings today:

Thursday 27th June 2019

My manifesting mantra for today:

AM
9
10
11
12
1
2
3
4
5
PM

What am I missing or just not seeing, right now?

Would I like to spend quality time with me?

What do I need to learn but won't admit to?

My thoughts and feelings today:

My manifesting mantra for today:

AM
9
10
11
12
1
2
3
4
5
PM

What feelings dominated my experience of life this month?

What feelings do I want to experience in the month to come?

Am I proud of who I am, how I behave and what I offer to this world?

My thoughts and feelings today:

Saturday 29th June 2019

My manifesting mantra for today:

AM

9

10

11

12

1

2

3

4

5

PM

What happened in the past month that made me feel good?

What happened in the past month that made me feel negative?

Am I living a life that is meaningful to me?

My thoughts and feelings today:

Sunday 30th June 2019

My manifesting mantra for today:

AM
9
10
11
12
1
2
3
4
5
PM

What were my happiest moments in the past month?

Have I made changes for the better this month?

How do I feel about my progress this month?

My thoughts and feelings today:

Monday 1st July 2019

My manifesting mantra for today:

AM

9

10

11

12

1

2

3

4

5

PM

My goal for July:

Reward if/when achieved:

My priorities this week:

My thoughts and feelings today:

Tuesday 2nd July 2019

My manifesting mantra for today:

AM

9

10

11

12

1

2

3

4

5

PM

Make a wish – it's a new moon today:

A small step I will take this week towards one of my life goals:

What am I happy about in my life right now?

My thoughts and feelings today:

Wednesday 3rd July 2019

My manifesting mantra for today:

AM
9
10
11
12
1
2
3
4
5
PM

Have I accepted my body as it is? Am I happy with the way I look?

How highly do I rate the importance of appearance and why?

Try eating for hunger and nutritional value only. Write down other times when you want to eat and why:

My thoughts and feelings today:

Thursday 4th July 2019

My manifesting mantra for today:

AM
9
10
11
12
1
2
3
4
5
PM

What is my passion in life or what things make me happy?

What about it makes me feel happiness?

How can I dedicate time to these pursuits of happiness?

My thoughts and feelings today:

Friday 5th July 2019

My manifesting mantra for today:

AM

9

10

11

12

1

2

3

4

5

PM

How has my energy vibration flowed this week?

What has worked well or not worked well this week?

How can I take a small step towards my best case scenario for this year?

My thoughts and feelings today:

"Eliminate all doubt and replace it with the full expectation that you will receive what you are asking for" - Rhona Byrne

Saturday 6th July 2019

My manifesting mantra for today:

AM
9
10
11
12
1
2
3
4
5
PM

What small things can I do to live my life to the fullest, today?

Am I enjoying my life's journey so far?

I am lucky because:

My thoughts and feelings today:

My manifesting mantra for today:

AM

9

10

11

12

1

2

3

4

5

PM

Something that inspired or touched you recently:

How have I made progress towards my life goals this week?

Have you experienced any blessings in disguise lately? Something that didn't turn out as you'd hoped, yet turned out for the best.

My thoughts and feelings today:

Monday 8th July 2019

My manifesting mantra for today:

AM
9
10
11
12
1
2
3
4
5
PM

A small step I will take this week towards one of my life goals:

My priorities this week:

Remember and note down a moment when you felt loved:

My thoughts and feelings today:

Tuesday 9th July 2019

My manifesting mantra for today:

AM
9
10
11
12
1
2
3
4
5
PM

Who is important to me?

I appreciate this person in my life because:

Something nice I can do for them this week:

My thoughts and feelings today:

"Let us be grateful to people who make us happy, the charming gardeners who make our souls blossom" - Marcel Proust

Wednesday 10th July 2019

My manifesting mantra for today:

AM
9
10
11
12
1
2
3
4
5
PM

Choose a love/family/friendship relationship in your life:

What kind of person am I like in this relationship?

How can I improve my actions to make the relationship better?

My thoughts and feelings today:

Thursday 11th July 2019

My manifesting mantra for today:

AM
9
10
11
12
1
2
3
4
5
PM

My random acts of kindness:

How have other people impacted your life recently?

How did their actions make you feel and what was your response?

My thoughts and feelings today:

Friday 12th July 2019

My manifesting mantra for today:

AM

9

10

11

12

1

2

3

4

5

PM

What did I learn so far this week?

If you did not receive what you wanted this week, can you identify something you received that is worth having?

Something I can do this weekend just for me:

My thoughts and feelings today:

Saturday 13th July 2019

My manifesting mantra for today:

AM
9
10
11
12
1
2
3
4
5
PM

What have I given to the people in my life today?

What have I received from the people in my life today?

Does the give and take flow in my relationships feel equal?

My thoughts and feelings today:

Sunday 14th July 2019

My manifesting mantra for today:

AM

9

10

11

12

1

2

3

4

5

PM

How have I made progress towards my life goals this week?

Three things I am grateful for:

1.

2.

3.

My thoughts and feelings today:

Monday 15th July 2019

My manifesting mantra for today:

AM

9

10

11

12

1

2

3

4

5

PM

My daily work goal to achieve this week:

What can I do today to achieve my daily work goal?

Reward if/when my daily work goal is achieved:

My thoughts and feelings today:

Tuesday 16th July 2019

My manifesting mantra for today:

AM
9
10
11
12
1
2
3
4
5
PM

Take a moment today to release any negative tension you have felt recently. Holding negative thoughts within makes you suffer, so take positive action. Change the situation, or find a way to accept and let it go. Note down any thoughts that come to mind.

My thoughts and feelings today:

Wednesday 17th July 2019

My manifesting mantra for today:

AM
9
10
11
12
1
2
3
4
5
PM

Practise being present and improving your focus. When we are truly in the moment, we are productive and time flies by. This is the ideal mind set for work! Each moment we experience is all we have; the past is gone, the future yet to come. Making the most of this moment, whether it be at work, with your family or a daily chore, is the key to making the most of your life.

My thoughts and feelings today:

Thursday 18th July 2019

My manifesting mantra for today:

AM

9

10

11

12

1

2

3

4

5

PM

In terms of my daily work, where do I see myself in two years?

If anything was possible where would I like to see myself in two years?

What can I do now to meet my expectations for the future?

My thoughts and feelings today:

Friday 19th July 2019

My manifesting mantra for today:

AM

9

10

11

12

1

2

3

4

5

PM

What went well this week?

What didn't go so well?

What have I learnt from those experiences?

My thoughts and feelings today:

Saturday 20th July 2019

My manifesting mantra for today:

AM

9

10

11

12

1

2

3

4

5

PM

How have I been using my free time lately?

Has that helped me to feel inspired, vibrant, healthy and fulfilled?

What changes could I make to feel more fulfilled in my life?

My thoughts and feelings today:

Sunday 21st July 2019

My manifesting mantra for today:

AM
9
10
11
12
1
2
3
4
5
PM

Have I made progress towards or achieved my daily work goal?

If so, how? If not, why?

One thing I have enjoyed about my daily work recently:

My thoughts and feelings today:

Monday 22nd July 2019

My manifesting mantra for today:

AM
9
10
11
12
1
2
3
4
5
PM

My goal for the week ahead:

That will help me achieve my life goal of:

My priorities this week:

My thoughts and feelings today:

Tuesday 23rd July 2019

My manifesting mantra for today:

AM
9
10
11
12
1
2
3
4
5
PM

How do I nurture my spiritual wellbeing?

What is important to me?

Do I spend enough time focusing on these things?

My thoughts and feelings today:

Wednesday 24th July 2019

My manifesting mantra for today:

AM
9
10
11
12
1
2
3
4
5
PM

Did I follow my intuition today and what did it tell me?

Practise connecting to your intuition: clear your mind, take three deep breaths, ask a question and trust the first thought that comes into your head. Note down the question and answer here:

Question:

Answer:

My thoughts and feelings today:

Thursday 25th July 2019

My manifesting mantra for today:

AM
9
10
11
12
1
2
3
4
5
PM

Practise the art of manifesting. Choose something small, sit back and observe how the Universe picks up on it. Little signs will appear around you. A song on the radio, something you see...

Write down your manifesting thought:

Note down the signs you receive:

My thoughts and feelings today:

"If you desire a glorious future, transform the present" - Patanjali

Friday 26th July 2019

My manifesting mantra for today:

AM
9
10
11
12
1
2
3
4
5
PM

What have I learnt so far this week?

Did I allow things to flow this week without trying to control the outcome?

Do something to invest in your happiness and wellbeing this weekend:

My thoughts and feelings today:

Saturday 27th July 2019

My manifesting mantra for today:

AM
9
10
11
12
1
2
3
4
5
PM

Do I contribute unconditional love in the life of others?

Do I practice 'self-love' or 'self-loathing'?

Be kind to yourself. Give yourself a compliment:

My thoughts and feelings today:

Sunday 28th July 2019

My manifesting mantra for today:

AM

9

10

11

12

1

2

3

4

5

PM

Have I made progress towards or achieved my weekly goal?

If so, how? If not, why?

Things I am grateful for from this week:

My thoughts and feelings today:

Monday 29th July 2019

My manifesting mantra for today:

AM

9

10

11

12

1

2

3

4

5

PM

A small step I will take this week towards one of my life goals:

My priorities this week:

Remember a moment when I put someone else's needs first:

My thoughts and feelings today:

Tuesday 30th July 2019

My manifesting mantra for today:

AM
9
10
11
12
1
2
3
4
5
PM

What are my top achievements this month?

What obstacles or fears did I experience this month?

What actions can I take to improve?

My thoughts and feelings today:

Wednesday 31st July 2019

My manifesting mantra for today:

AM
9
10
11
12
1
2
3
4
5
PM

What happened in the past month that made me feel good?

What happened in the past month that made me feel negative?

Am I happy with the way I spent my time this month?

My thoughts and feelings today:

Thursday 1st August 2019

My manifesting mantra for today:

AM
9
10
11
12
1
2
3
4
5
PM

Make a wish – it's a new moon today:

My goal for August:

Reward if/when achieved:

My thoughts and feelings today:

"Yesterday is not ours to recover, but tomorrow is ours to win or lose"
- Lyndon B. Johnson

Friday 2nd August 2019

My manifesting mantra for today:

AM
9
10
11
12
1
2
3
4
5
PM

A small step I will take this week towards one of my life goals:

What am I happy about in my life right now?

Something I can do this weekend, just for me, to make me happy:

My thoughts and feelings today:

Saturday 3rd August 2019

My manifesting mantra for today:

AM
9
10
11
12
1
2
3
4
5
PM

Visualise your ideal life and describe here:

How can you bring your ideal life into your everyday life:

What small step can you take now to bring your ideal life into reality:

My thoughts and feelings today:

Sunday 4th August 2019

My manifesting mantra for today:

AM
9
10
11
12
1
2
3
4
5
PM

Review the twenty life goals at the start of the journal. Have any of these changed?

Why?

Do I have any new ones?

My thoughts and feelings today:

Monday 5th August 2019

My manifesting mantra for today:

AM
9
10
11
12
1
2
3
4
5
PM

A small step I will take this week towards one of my life goals:

My priorities this week:

Remember and note down a moment when you felt truly happy:

My thoughts and feelings today:

Tuesday 6th August 2019

My manifesting mantra for today:

AM

9

10

11

12

1

2

3

4

5

PM

What about today was better than yesterday?

What makes my heart skip a beat?

What negative habits do I have that I know I need to let go of?

My thoughts and feelings today:

Wednesday 7th August 2019

My manifesting mantra for today:

AM
9
10
11
12
1
2
3
4
5
PM

How helpful have your morning and evening rituals been?

What other things do you do each day to keep yourself grounded?

How can you help those around you to relax and destress?

My thoughts and feelings today:

Thursday 8th August 2019

My manifesting mantra for today:

AM
9
10
11
12
1
2
3
4
5
PM

Who's needs do I consider day to day?

How well do I prioritise my needs against the needs of others?

Am I dedicating enough time to the pursuit of my happiness?

My thoughts and feelings today:

Friday 9th August 2019

My manifesting mantra for today:

AM
9
10
11
12
1
2
3
4
5
PM

How has my energy vibration flowed this week?

What has worked well or not worked well this week?

How can I take a small step towards my best case scenario for this year? How has it changed?

My thoughts and feelings today:

Saturday 10th August 2019

My manifesting mantra for today:

AM
9
10
11
12
1
2
3
4
5
PM

Something I can do today to add to my quality of life:

Am I enjoying my life's journey so far?

My favourite song at the moment and how it makes me feel:

My thoughts and feelings today:

"I attract to my life whatever I give my attention, energy and focus to, whether positive or negative" - Michael Losier

Sunday 11th August 2019

My manifesting mantra for today:

AM
9
10
11
12
1
2
3
4
5
PM

How did I make myself feel good this week?

How have I made progress towards my life goals this week?

What can I do to make next week better than this one?

My thoughts and feelings today:

Monday 12th August 2019

My manifesting mantra for today:

AM
9
10
11
12
1
2
3
4
5
PM

A small step I will take this week towards one of my life goals:

My priorities this week:

Something kind or thoughtful someone did for you lately:

My thoughts and feelings today:

Tuesday 13th August 2019

My manifesting mantra for today:

AM
9
10
11
12
1
2
3
4
5
PM

Are my actions consistent with what I say?

What culture do I want to create with my friends? Culture being the traditions, habits, practices and values you have.

Are there relationships that I need to repair or let go?

My thoughts and feelings today:

Wednesday 14th August 2019

My manifesting mantra for today:

AM

9

10

11

12

1

2

3

4

5

PM

Choose a love/family/friendship relationship in your life:

Would I want to be the other person in this relationship with me?

How can I improve my actions to make the relationship better?

My thoughts and feelings today:

Thursday 15th August 2019

My manifesting mantra for today:

AM
9
10
11
12
1
2
3
4
5
PM

Write down something you would like to release from your life:
What emotions need to be healed? Who needs to be forgiven?
What relationships no longer serve you?

Take three deep breaths and say out loud or in your head: "I release ....". Let all the negativity drain away by forgiving the situation or person who wronged you and thank the Universe for taking care of the situation on your behalf.

My thoughts and feelings today:

Friday 16th August 2019

My manifesting mantra for today:

AM
9
10
11
12
1
2
3
4
5
PM

What did I learn so far this week?

Did I allow things to flow this week without trying to control the outcome?

Something I can do this weekend just for me:

My thoughts and feelings today:

"You must be the change you wish to see in the world" - Ghandi

Saturday 17th August 2019

My manifesting mantra for today:

AM

9

10

11

12

1

2

3

4

5

PM

Which relationship in my life needs more of my attention and love right now?

Is there any relationship in my life that is toxic or any person who drains my sense of self?

Recognise the difference between the two relationships above and dedicate your time to those who deserve it.

My thoughts and feelings today:

Sunday 18th August 2019

My manifesting mantra for today:

AM

9

10

11

12

1

2

3

4

5

PM

How have I made progress towards my life goals this week?

My gratitude list this week:

1.

2.

3.

My thoughts and feelings today:

Monday 19th August 2019

My manifesting mantra for today:

AM

9

10

11

12

1

2

3

4

5

PM

My daily work goal to achieve this week:

What can I do today to achieve my daily work goal?

Reward if/when my daily work goal is achieved:

My thoughts and feelings today:

Tuesday 20th August 2019

My manifesting mantra for today:

AM

9

10

11

12

1

2

3

4

5

PM

How is my emotional vibration today?

How has my emotional vibration fluctuated this month?

How can I improve my emotional vibration day to day?

My thoughts and feelings today:

Wednesday 21st August 2019

My manifesting mantra for today:

AM

9

10

11

12

1

2

3

4

5

PM

A simple mindfulness exercise to increase your awareness and to be present in the moment: take a deep breath in and while you hold it, look around you and notice something you can see, feel, hear, smell, taste. Use all five senses to experience the moment you are in. You can do this anywhere, anytime. Place your hand on your heart and feel your heartbeat. Let the answers your seek come from within.

My thoughts and feelings today:

Thursday 22nd August 2019

My manifesting mantra for today:

AM
9
10
11
12
1
2
3
4
5
PM

What do I do in my life that I know is not working for me?

What do I do in my life that I know does work for me?

What do I need to change in my life to get the results I want?

My thoughts and feelings today:

Friday 23rd August 2019

My manifesting mantra for today:

AM

9

10

11

12

1

2

3

4

5

PM

What have I learnt so far this week?

Is there anything I intended to achieve that did not happen? Why?

What I am looking forward to this weekend:

My thoughts and feelings today:

Saturday 24th August 2019

My manifesting mantra for today:

AM
9
10
11
12
1
2
3
4
5
PM

How do I take time out from work to relax?

Do I have a good work life balance?

What can I do to improve my work life balance?

My thoughts and feelings today:

Sunday 25th August 2019

My manifesting mantra for today:

AM
9
10
11
12
1
2
3
4
5
PM

Have I made progress towards or achieved my daily work goal?

If so, how? If not, why?

My reflections from this week are:

My thoughts and feelings today:

Monday 26th August 2019

My manifesting mantra for today:

AM
9
10
11
12
1
2
3
4
5
PM

My goal for the week ahead:

That will help me achieve my life goal of:

My priorities this week:

My thoughts and feelings today:

"To bring anything into your life, imagine that it's already there." ~ *Richard Bach*

Tuesday 27th August 2019

My manifesting mantra for today:

AM
9
10
11
12
1
2
3
4
5
PM

What have I been day dreaming about lately?

Have I spent time focusing my thoughts on positivity and what I want to happen?

Has the Universe given me any signs that it is listening?

My thoughts and feelings today:

Wednesday 28th August 2019

My manifesting mantra for today:

AM
9
10
11
12
1
2
3
4
5
PM

Am I feeling more connected to my intuition?

Practise connecting to your intuition: clear your mind, take three deep breaths, ask a question and trust the first thought that comes into your head. Note down the question and answer here:

Question:

Answer:

My thoughts and feelings today:

Thursday 29th August 2019

My manifesting mantra for today:

AM
9
10
11
12
1
2
3
4
5
PM

Am I connected to Mother Nature around me?

How can I spend more time connecting with Mother Nature?

What small thing can I do to help our world?

My thoughts and feelings today:

Friday 30th August 2019

My manifesting mantra for today:

AM

9

10

11

12

1

2

3

4

5

PM

Make a wish – it's a new moon today:

What would I like to happen in my life next month?

What is within my power that I can do to make it more likely to happen?

My thoughts and feelings today:

Saturday 31st August 2019

My manifesting mantra for today:

AM
9
10
11
12
1
2
3
4
5
PM

What were my happiest moments in the past month?

What obstacles or fears did I experience this month?

How do I feel about my progress this month?

My thoughts and feelings today:

Sunday 1st September 2019

My manifesting mantra for today:

AM
9
10
11
12
1
2
3
4
5
PM

My goal for September:

Reward if/when achieved:

My priorities this week:

My thoughts and feelings today:

Monday 2nd September 2019

My manifesting mantra for today:

AM
9
10
11
12
1
2
3
4
5
PM

A small step I will take this week towards one of my life goals:

My priorities this week:

Something I will do this week, just for me, to make me happy:

My thoughts and feelings today:

"Happiness lies in the joy of achievement and the thrill of creative effort" - Franklin D. Roosevelt

Tuesday 3rd September 2019

My manifesting mantra for today:

AM
9
10
11
12
1
2
3
4
5
PM

What am I happy about in my life right now?

Something new I would like to do that would make me happy:

A person in my life who makes me happy and why:

My thoughts and feelings today:

Wednesday 4th September 2019

My manifesting mantra for today:

AM
9
10
11
12
1
2
3
4
5
PM

How deeply am I connected with my heart?

What is my deepest fear?

Create a positive affirmation to rewire your mind against it:

My thoughts and feelings today:

Thursday 5th September 2019

My manifesting mantra for today:

AM
9
10
11
12
1
2
3
4
5
PM

What is my definition of a happy life:

Do I feel that I have a happy life?

Practical things I can do to choose happiness:

My thoughts and feelings today:

Friday 6th September 2019

My manifesting mantra for today:

AM
9
10
11
12
1
2
3
4
5
PM

How has my energy vibration flowed this week?

What has worked well or not worked well this week?

How can I take a small step towards my best case scenario for this year?

My thoughts and feelings today:

Saturday 7th September 2019

My manifesting mantra for today:

AM

9

10

11

12

1

2

3

4

5

PM

What small things can I do to live my life to the fullest, today?

Am I enjoying my life's journey so far?

I am lucky because:

My thoughts and feelings today:

Sunday 8th September 2019

My manifesting mantra for today:

AM
9
10
11
12
1
2
3
4
5
PM

How did I make myself feel good this week?

How have I made progress towards my life goals this week?

What can I do to make next week better than this one?

My thoughts and feelings today:

Monday 9th September 2019

My manifesting mantra for today:

AM
9
10
11
12
1
2
3
4
5
PM

A small step I will take this week towards one of my life goals:

My priorities this week:

What kind or thoughtful thing did someone do for you lately:

My thoughts and feelings today:

Tuesday 10th September 2019

My manifesting mantra for today:

AM
9
10
11
12
1
2
3
4
5
PM

Who is important to me?

I appreciate this person in my life because:

Something nice I can do for them this week:

My thoughts and feelings today:

Wednesday 11th September 2019

My manifesting mantra for today:

AM
9
10
11
12
1
2
3
4
5
PM

Choose a love/family/friendship relationship in your life:

What kind of person am I like in this relationship?

How can I improve my actions to make the relationship better?

My thoughts and feelings today:

Thursday 12th September 2019

My manifesting mantra for today:

AM

9

10

11

12

1

2

3

4

5

PM

My random acts of kindness:

How have other people impacted your life today?

How did their actions make you feel and what was your response?

My thoughts and feelings today:

Friday 13th September 2019

My manifesting mantra for today:

AM

9

10

11

12

1

2

3

4

5

PM

What did I learn so far this week?

What non-physical gifts have you received recently - someone's time, attention, support?

Who have you enjoyed being around recently, and why?

My thoughts and feelings today:

Friday 13th is usually lucky for me, may this day bring you good luck too!

Saturday 14th September 2019

My manifesting mantra for today:

AM

9

10

11

12

1

2

3

4

5

PM

Imagine the full moon as the end of a phase and celebrate all of the wonderful things that have happened during this time, however small. Take time to go outside and admire its beauty. Mention everything that you are grateful for and then set your intentions for what you would like the Universe to bring to your life for the month to come. Say it out loud and let the Universe take care of it. Record your intentions below:

Your thoughts and feelings today:

Sunday 15th September 2019

My manifesting mantra for today:

AM
9
10
11
12
1
2
3
4
5
PM

How have I made progress towards my life goals this week?

Three things I am grateful for:
1.
2.
3.

My thoughts and feelings today:

Monday 16^h September 2019

My manifesting mantra for today:

AM
9
10
11
12
1
2
3
4
5
PM

My daily work goal to achieve this week:

What can I do today to achieve my daily work goal?

Reward if/when my daily work goal is achieved:

My thoughts and feelings today:

Tuesday 17th September 2019

My manifesting mantra for today:

AM

9

10

11

12

1

2

3

4

5

PM

Am I feeling professionally fulfilled in my daily work?

What would I most like to learn in the next 12 months?

What are my strengths and achievements in the past year that I can celebrate?

My thoughts and feelings today:

"Communication, the human connection, is the key to personal and career success" - Paul J. Meyer

Wednesday 18th September 2019

My manifesting mantra for today:

AM
9
10
11
12
1
2
3
4
5
PM

I was once told that when you meditate you become an observer of the mind; you observe the thoughts and emotions of your brain as if you are an external entity. Take a step back and observe how your emotions ebb and flow or flare up throughout each day. When you feel emotions taking over, stop and smile. Become aware of the immediate physiological response in your body and take back control of your mind. Choose happiness.

My thoughts and feelings today:

Thursday 19th September 2019

My manifesting mantra for today:

AM

9

10

11

12

1

2

3

4

5

PM

What should I read to expand my horizons?

What new challenge should I undertake?

Who is my role model and why?

My thoughts and feelings today:

"We don't stop playing because we grow old; we grow old because we stop playing" - George Bernard Shaw

Friday 20th September 2019

My manifesting mantra for today:

AM

9

10

11

12

1

2

3

4

5

PM

How has my energy vibration flowed this week?

What has worked well or not worked well this week?

How can I take a small step towards my best case scenario for this year?

My thoughts and feelings today:

Saturday 21st September 2019

My manifesting mantra for today:

AM
9
10
11
12
1
2
3
4
5
PM

How do I use my free time?

Has that helped me to feel inspired, vibrant, healthy and fulfilled?

What changes could I make to feel more fulfilled in my life?

My thoughts and feelings today:

Sunday 22nd September 2019

My manifesting mantra for today:

AM

9

10

11

12

1

2

3

4

5

PM

Have I made progress towards or achieved my daily work goal?

If so, how? If not, why?

My reflections from this week are:

My thoughts and feelings today:

Monday 23rd September 2019

My manifesting mantra for today:

AM

9

10

11

12

1

2

3

4

5

PM

My goal for the week ahead:

That will help me achieve my life goal of:

My priorities this week:

My thoughts and feelings today:

Tuesday 24th September 2019

My manifesting mantra for today:

AM
9
10
11
12
1
2
3
4
5
PM

How has today contributed to the grand scheme of my life?

How can I find ways to appreciate each day I am blessed to have?

Remember and note down a moment when you felt connected to nature / the universe / life's source:

My thoughts and feelings today:

Wednesday 25th September 2019

My manifesting mantra for today:

AM
9
10
11
12
1
2
3
4
5
PM

Write down a moment when your intuition was right:

Practise connecting to your intuition: clear your mind, take three deep breaths, ask a question and trust the first thought that comes into your head. Note down the question and answer here:

Question:

Answer:

My thoughts and feelings today:

Thursday 26th September 2019

My manifesting mantra for today:

AM

9

10

11

12

1

2

3

4

5

PM

My current habits for eating, drinking and exercising:

Are my current habits working for me or against me?

How can I change my habits to work for me?

My thoughts and feelings today:

"The food you eat can be either the safest and most powerful form of medicine or the slowest form of poison" Ann Wigmore

Friday 27th September 2019

My manifesting mantra for today:

AM
9
10
11
12
1
2
3
4
5
PM

Practise the art of manifesting. Choose something small, sit back and observe how the Universe picks up on it. Little signs will appear around you. A song on the radio, something you see...

Write down your manifesting thought:

Note down the signs you receive:

My thoughts and feelings today:

Saturday 28th September 2019

My manifesting mantra for today:

AM

9

10

11

12

1

2

3

4

5

PM

Make a wish – it's a new moon today:

What happened in the past month that made me feel good?

Am I living a life that is meaningful to me?

My thoughts and feelings today:

My manifesting mantra for today:

AM

9

10

11

12

1

2

3

4

5

PM

What were my happiest moments in the past month?

What obstacles or fears did I experience this month?

How do I feel about my progress this month?

My thoughts and feelings today:

Monday 30th September 2019

My manifesting mantra for today:

AM

9

10

11

12

1

2

3

4

5

PM

What feelings dominated my experience of life this month?

What feelings do I want to experience in the month to come?

Am I proud of who I am, how I behave and what I offer to this world?

My thoughts and feelings today:

Tuesday 1st October 2019

My manifesting mantra for today:

AM

9

10

11

12

1

2

3

4

5

PM

My goal for October:

Reward if/when achieved:

My priorities this week:

My thoughts and feelings today:

Wednesday 2nd October 2019

My manifesting mantra for today:

AM
9
10
11
12
1
2
3
4
5
PM

Something I will do this week, just for me, to make me happy:

If you had an extra hour in the day, what would you do with it?

When was the last time you felt most excited or alive?

My thoughts and feelings today:

Thursday 3rd October 2019

My manifesting mantra for today:

AM
9
10
11
12
1
2
3
4
5
PM

What small changes could you make to improve your day?

What is something that always makes you smile?

Am I dedicating enough time to the pursuit of my happiness?

My thoughts and feelings today:

"Change is the very essence of life and we can allow this change to empower us" - Maya Fiennes

Friday 4th October 2019

My manifesting mantra for today:

AM

9

10

11

12

1

2

3

4

5

PM

How has my energy vibration flowed this week?

What has worked well or not worked well this week?

How can I take a small step towards my best case scenario for this year?

My thoughts and feelings today:

Saturday 5th October 2019

My manifesting mantra for today:

AM

9

10

11

12

1

2

3

4

5

PM

Something I can do today to enhance my quality of life:

Am I enjoying my life's journey so far?

I am lucky because:

My thoughts and feelings today:

Sunday 6th October 2019

My manifesting mantra for today:

AM
9
10
11
12
1
2
3
4
5
PM

How did I make myself feel good this week?

How have I made progress towards my life goals this week?

What can I do to make next week better than this one?

My thoughts and feelings today:

Monday 7th October 2019

My manifesting mantra for today:

AM
9
10
11
12
1
2
3
4
5
PM

A small step I will take this week towards one of my life goals:

My priorities this week:

Who is always there for you, and how do you feel about them?

My thoughts and feelings today:

Tuesday 8th October 2019

My manifesting mantra for today:

AM
9
10
11
12
1
2
3
4
5
PM

Who is important to me?

I appreciate this person in my life because:

Something nice I can do for them this week:

My thoughts and feelings today:

"Being deeply loved by someone gives you strength, while loving someone deeply gives you courage" - Lao Tzu

Wednesday 9th October 2019

My manifesting mantra for today:

AM

9

10

11

12

1

2

3

4

5

PM

How often do I compliment others?

How can I improve my attentiveness and listening?

How do I want to be remembered?

My thoughts and feelings today:

Thursday 10th October 2019

My manifesting mantra for today:

AM
9
10
11
12
1
2
3
4
5
PM

My random acts of kindness:

How have other people impacted your life lately?

How did their actions make you feel and what was your response?

My thoughts and feelings today:

Friday 11th October 2019

My manifesting mantra for today:

AM
9
10
11
12
1
2
3
4
5
PM

What was my soul's lesson this week?

Who are the five people I spend the most time with?

Are these people enabling me or holding me back?

My thoughts and feelings today:

Saturday 12th October 2019

My manifesting mantra for today:

AM

9

10

11

12

1

2

3

4

5

PM

How do I positively affect the lives of those around me?

How often do I laugh and make others laugh?

Have I been involved in an argument lately and what did I achieve? Was it worth it?

My thoughts and feelings today:

Sunday 13th October 2019

My manifesting mantra for today:

AM
9
10
11
12
1
2
3
4
5
PM

Spend five minutes today thinking about all the positive things in your life and write them below. Thank the Universe for all you have. Look in the mirror and say nice things to yourself! During a full moon your positive thoughts will be energised and multiplied.

My thoughts and feelings today:

Monday 14th October 2019

My manifesting mantra for today:

AM
9
10
11
12
1
2
3
4
5
PM

My daily work goal to achieve this week:

What can I do today to achieve my daily work goal?

Reward if/when my daily work goal is achieved:

My thoughts and feelings today:

Tuesday 15th October 2019

My manifesting mantra for today:

AM

9

10

11

12

1

2

3

4

5

PM

What do I do in my life that I know is not working for me?

What do I do in my life that I know does work for me?

What do I need to change in my life to get the results I want?

My thoughts and feelings today:

Wednesday 16th October 2019

My manifesting mantra for today:

AM

9

10

11

12

1

2

3

4

5

PM

What was a doing a year ago?

Would I be happy with what I am doing now?

What do I want to be doing a year from now?

My thoughts and feelings today:

Thursday 17th October 2019

My manifesting mantra for today:

AM

9

10

11

12

1

2

3

4

5

PM

What are my ambitions?

Am I on route to realising my ambitions?

What do I want to learn next?

My thoughts and feelings today:

Friday 18th October 2019

My manifesting mantra for today:

AM
9
10
11
12
1
2
3
4
5
PM

What went well this week?

What didn't go so well?

What have I learnt from those experiences?

My thoughts and feelings today:

Saturday 19th October 2019

My manifesting mantra for today:

AM
9
10
11
12
1
2
3
4
5
PM

Practise the art of manifesting. Choose something small, sit back and observe how the Universe picks up on it. Little signs will appear around you. A song on the radio, something you see...

Write down your manifesting thought:

Note down the signs you receive:

My thoughts and feelings today:

Sunday 20th October 2019

My manifesting mantra for today:

AM
9
10
11
12
1
2
3
4
5
PM

Have I made progress towards or achieved my daily work goal?

If so, how? If not, why?

Something that made me smile recently:

My thoughts and feelings today:

Monday 21st October 2019

My manifesting mantra for today:

AM
9
10
11
12
1
2
3
4
5
PM

My goal for the week ahead:

That will help me achieve my life goal of:

My priorities this week:

My thoughts and feelings today:

Tuesday 22nd October 2019

My manifesting mantra for today:

AM
9
10
11
12
1
2
3
4
5
PM

What one thing would bring me more satisfaction in my life?

What have I done in the past month to attain it?

What will I do in the next month to attain it?

My thoughts and feelings today:

Wednesday 23rd October 2019

My manifesting mantra for today:

AM
9
10
11
12
1
2
3
4
5
PM

How would I describe myself?

What qualities do I want to embody?

Love your essence, what makes you YOU, but know that you can make positive choices to develop different aspects of your soul.

My thoughts and feelings today:

Thursday 24th October 2019

My manifesting mantra for today:

AM
9
10
11
12
1
2
3
4
5
PM

What is my bucket list? Three things I want to do before I die:

1.
2.
3.

How would I spend the next day if it were my last:

My thoughts and feelings today:

Friday 25th October 2019

My manifesting mantra for today:

AM
9
10
11
12
1
2
3
4
5
PM

How has my energy vibration flowed this week?

Was I led by my emotions or did I observe and take control?

How can I take a small step towards my best case scenario for this year?

My thoughts and feelings today:

"Be kind whenever possible. It is always possible" - Dalai Lama

Saturday 26th October 2019

My manifesting mantra for today:

AM
9
10
11
12
1
2
3
4
5
PM

What or whom did I make better today?

Has that helped me to feel inspired, vibrant, healthy and fulfilled?

What small thing can I start doing to be of service to the world?

My thoughts and feelings today:

Sunday 27th October 2019

My manifesting mantra for today:

AM

9

10

11

12

1

2

3

4

5

PM

Have I made progress towards or achieved my goal this week?

If so, how? If not, why?

I am grateful for:

My thoughts and feelings today:

Monday 28th October 2019

My manifesting mantra for today:

AM

9

10

11

12

1

2

3

4

5

PM

Make a wish – it's a new moon today:

A small step I will take this week towards one of my life goals:

My priorities this week:

My thoughts and feelings today?

Tuesday 29th October 2019

My manifesting mantra for today:

AM

9

10

11

12

1

2

3

4

5

PM

Am I living the life I chose for myself – or someone else's ideal?

Am I spending my time on what I value most?

Is there anything I can change day to day to be happier?

My thoughts and feelings today:

"Life becomes more meaningful when you realise the simple fact that you'll never get the same moment twice" - Amy Rees Anderson

Wednesday 30th October 2019

My manifesting mantra for today:

AM

9

10

11

12

1

2

3

4

5

PM

What were my happiest moments in the past month?

What negative emotions did I experience this month?

How do I feel about my progress this month?

My thoughts and feelings today:

Halloween

Thursday 31st October 2019

My manifesting mantra for today:

AM

9

10

11

12

1

2

3

4

5

PM

What are my top achievements this month?

Am I happy with how I used my time this month?

What was my soul's lesson this month?

My thoughts and feelings today:

Friday 1st November 2019

My manifesting mantra for today:

AM
9
10
11
12
1
2
3
4
5
PM

My goal for November:

Reward if/when achieved:

What is the best possible situation at the end of this month?

My thoughts and feelings today:

Saturday 2nd November 2019

My manifesting mantra for today:

AM

9

10

11

12

1

2

3

4

5

PM

What things in my life have made me feel happy lately?

How can I dedicate more of my time to these pursuits?

Create something to look forward to next week:

My thoughts and feelings today:

Sunday 3rd November 2019

My manifesting mantra for today:

AM
9
10
11
12
1
2
3
4
5
PM

Something that inspired or touched you recently:

How have I made progress towards my life goals this week?

Have you experienced any blessings in disguise lately? Something that didn't turn out as you'd hoped, yet turned out for the best.

My thoughts and feelings today:

Monday 4th November 2019

My manifesting mantra for today:

AM

9

10

11

12

1

2

3

4

5

PM

A small step I will take this week towards one of my life goals:

My priorities this week:

Who have you enjoyed being around recently, and why?

My thoughts and feelings today:

"Spread love everywhere you go. Let no one ever come to you without leaving happier" - Mother Teresa

Tuesday 5th November 2019

My manifesting mantra for today:

AM
9
10
11
12
1
2
3
4
5
PM

Who is important to me?

I appreciate this person in my life because:

Something nice I can do for them this week:

My thoughts and feelings today:

Wednesday 6th November 2019

My manifesting mantra for today:

AM
9
10
11
12
1
2
3
4
5
PM

Do I tell those I love that I love them?

Are the boundaries I have set with others the right ones?

Where should I be a more positive influence?

My thoughts and feelings today:

"We waste time looking for the perfect lover instead of creating the perfect love" - Tom Robbins

Thursday 7th November 2019

My manifesting mantra for today:

AM
9
10
11
12
1
2
3
4
5
PM

My random acts of kindness:

How have other people impacted your life today?

How did their actions make you feel and what was your response?

My thoughts and feelings today:

Friday 8th November 2019

My manifesting mantra for today:

AM
9
10
11
12
1
2
3
4
5
PM

What did I learn so far this week?

Did I allow things to flow this week without trying to control the outcome?

Something I can do this weekend just for me:

My thoughts and feelings today:

Saturday 9th November 2019

My manifesting mantra for today:

AM

9

10

11

12

1

2

3

4

5

PM

What qualities do I have that make me a good friend?

Are the people that demand my time the ones who I really want to spend my time with?

Do I make enough effort with my friends and do I feel valued in return?

My thoughts and feelings today:

Sunday 10th November 2019

My manifesting mantra for today:

AM
9
10
11
12
1
2
3
4
5
PM

How have I made progress towards my life goals this week?

My gratitude list this week:
1.
2.
3.

My thoughts and feelings today:

Monday 11th November 2019

My manifesting mantra for today:

AM
9
10
11
12
1
2
3
4
5
PM

My daily work goal to achieve this week:

What can I do today to achieve my daily work goal?

Reward if/when my daily work goal is achieved:

My thoughts and feelings today:

Tuesday 12th November 2019

My manifesting mantra for today:

AM
9
10
11
12
1
2
3
4
5
PM

Harness the energy of the full moon today and take a moment today to release any negative tension you have felt recently. Holding negative thoughts within makes you suffer, so take positive action. Change the situation, or find a way to accept and let it go. Note down any thoughts that come to mind.

My thoughts and feelings today:

Wednesday 13th November 2019

My manifesting mantra for today:

AM

9

10

11

12

1

2

3

4

5

PM

This month's mindfulness exercise is to question the emotions that you feel. Ask yourself, "am I really this feeling, this emotion, this thought?" Sometimes we get caught up in the moment and act out in a way that doesn't truly represent ourselves. Take time to observe your emotional reactions and question them. It may give you the opportunity to avoid saying or doing something you may regret or that doesn't embody your soul's true intention.

My thoughts and feelings today:

Thursday 14th November 2019

My manifesting mantra for today:

AM
9
10
11
12
1
2
3
4
5
PM

Three things I am grateful for that my daily work brings to my life and why?

1.

2.

3.

My thoughts and feelings today:

My manifesting mantra for today:

AM

9

10

11

12

1

2

3

4

5

PM

What went well this week?

What didn't go so well?

What have I learnt from those experiences?

My thoughts and feelings today:

Saturday 16th November 2019

My manifesting mantra for today:

AM

9

10

11

12

1

2

3

4

5

PM

Am I good at spending money or saving it?

How can I make changes to save or spend money more wisely?

Set a specific goal about saving or spending for next month:

My thoughts and feelings today:

Sunday 17th November 2019

My manifesting mantra for today:

AM

9

10

11

12

1

2

3

4

5

PM

Have I made progress towards or achieved my daily work goal?

If so, how? If not, why?

My reflections from this week are:

My thoughts and feelings today:

Monday 18th November 2019

My manifesting mantra for today:

AM
9
10
11
12
1
2
3
4
5
PM

My goal for the week ahead:

That will help me achieve my life goal of:

My priorities this week:

My thoughts and feelings today:

Tuesday 19th November 2019

My manifesting mantra for today:

AM

9

10

11

12

1

2

3

4

5

PM

What is the best thing in my life right now?

What is the worst thing in my life right now?

What would I like to happen in the next week?

My thoughts and feelings for today:

Wednesday 20th November 2019

My manifesting mantra for today:

AM
9
10
11
12
1
2
3
4
5
PM

Did I follow my intuition today and what did it tell me?

Practise connecting to your intuition: clear your mind, take three deep breaths, ask a question and trust the first thought that comes into your head. Note down the question and answer here:

Question:

Answer:

My thoughts and feelings today:

Thursday 21st November 2019

My manifesting mantra for today:

AM
9
10
11
12
1
2
3
4
5
PM

Three things that I worry about:
1.
2.
3.

Create positive affirmations to reprogram how you think about these worries:
1.
2.
3.

My thoughts and feelings today:

Friday 22nd November 2019

My manifesting mantra for today:

AM
9
10
11
12
1
2
3
4
5
PM

What have I learnt so far this week?

Did I allow things to flow this week without trying to control the outcome?

Do something to invest in your happiness and wellbeing this weekend:

My thoughts and feelings today:

Saturday 23rd November 2019

My manifesting mantra for today:

AM
9
10
11
12
1
2
3
4
5
PM

Is my body healthy?

What do I do that contributes to my health?

What do I do that works against my health?

My thoughts and feelings for today:

"To keep the body in good health is a duty ... otherwise we shall not be able to keep our mind strong and clear" - Buddha

Sunday 24th November 2019

My manifesting mantra for today:

AM

9

10

11

12

1

2

3

4

5

PM

Have I made progress towards or achieved my weekly goal?

If so, how? If not, why?

My gratitude list this week:

My thoughts and feelings today:

Monday 25th November 2019

My manifesting mantra for today:

AM
9
10
11
12
1
2
3
4
5
PM

My goal for the week ahead:

That will help me achieve my life goal of:

My priorities this week:

My thoughts and feelings today:

Tuesday 26th November 2019

My manifesting mantra for today:

AM

9

10

11

12

1

2

3

4

5

PM

Make a wish – it's a new moon today:

What am I looking forward to this week:

Something that made me laugh recently:

My thoughts and feelings today:

Wednesday 27th November 2019

My manifesting mantra for today:

AM
9
10
11
12
1
2
3
4
5
PM

Three words to describe my emotional vibration today:

How has my emotional vibration fluctuated over the past month?

How can I improve my emotional vibration day to day?

My thoughts and feelings today:

Thursday 28th November 2019

My manifesting mantra for today:

AM
9
10
11
12
1
2
3
4
5
PM

What small success have I achieved this week?

My gratitude list for the week:

1.
2.
3.
4.

My thoughts and feelings today:

Friday 29th November 2019

My manifesting mantra for today:

AM
9
10
11
12
1
2
3
4
5
PM

What happened in the past month that made me feel good?

What happened in the past month that made me feel negative?

Am I happy with the way I spent my time this month?

My thoughts and feelings today:

Saturday 30th November 2019

My manifesting mantra for today:

AM

9

10

11

12

1

2

3

4

5

PM

What's the best thing that happened in the past month?

How can I create similar experiences?

If I could have anything, what would I ask the Universe for?

My thoughts and feelings today:

Sunday 1st December 2019

My manifesting mantra for today:

AM
9
10
11
12
1
2
3
4
5
PM

My goal for December:

Reward if/when achieved:

How can I live my life to the fullest this month?

My thoughts and feelings today:

"The saddest summary of a life contains three descriptions: could have, might have and should have" - Louis E. Boone

Monday 2nd December 2019

My manifesting mantra for today:

AM

9

10

11

12

1

2

3

4

5

PM

A small step I will take this week towards one of my life goals:

My priorities this week:

Something I will do this week, just for me, to make me happy:

My thoughts and feelings today:

Tuesday 3rd December 2019

My manifesting mantra for today:

AM

9

10

11

12

1

2

3

4

5

PM

What am I happy about in my life right now?

Something new I would like to do that would make me happy:

A small step I will take this week towards one of my life goals:

My thoughts and feelings today:

Wednesday 4th December 2019

My manifesting mantra for today:

AM

9

10

11

12

1

2

3

4

5

PM

How important is routine to me and why?

How can I improve my morning ritual?

How can I improve my evening ritual?

My thoughts and feelings today:

Thursday 5th December 2019

My manifesting mantra for today:

AM
9
10
11
12
1
2
3
4
5
PM

How have I grown as a person over the last five years:

What key events in my life have had an impact on the person I am today:

My thoughts and feelings today:

Friday 6th December 2019

My manifesting mantra for today:

AM
9
10
11
12
1
2
3
4
5
PM

How has my energy vibration flowed this week?

What has worked well or not worked well this week?

How can I take a small step towards my best case scenario for this year? Has that scenario changed?

My thoughts and feelings today:

Saturday 7th December 2019

My manifesting mantra for today:

AM

9

10

11

12

1

2

3

4

5

PM

What small things can I do to live my life to the fullest, today?

Am I enjoying my life's journey so far?

I am lucky because:

My thoughts and feelings today:

Sunday 8th December 2019

My manifesting mantra for today:

AM
9
10
11
12
1
2
3
4
5
PM

How did I make myself feel good this week?

How have I made progress towards my life goals this week?

What can I do to make next week better than this one?

My thoughts and feelings today:

Monday 9th December 2019

My manifesting mantra for today:

AM

9

10

11

12

1

2

3

4

5

PM

A small step I will take this week towards one of my life goals:

My priorities this week:

Remember and note down a moment when you felt appreciated:

My thoughts and feelings today:

Tuesday 10th December 2019

My manifesting mantra for today:

AM
9
10
11
12
1
2
3
4
5
PM

Are my actions consistent with what I say?

How have my family and friendship cultures changed this year? Have I done anything to improve them?

Are there relationships that I need to repair or let go?

My thoughts and feelings today:

Wednesday 11th December 2019

My manifesting mantra for today:

AM
9
10
11
12
1
2
3
4
5
PM

Choose a love/family/friendship relationship in your life:

Would I want to be the other person in this relationship with me?

Something nice I can do for them this week:

My thoughts and feelings today:

Thursday 12th December 2019

My manifesting mantra for today:

AM
9
10
11
12
1
2
3
4
5
PM

Another lunar cycle, another opportunity to start again. Is there an aspect of your life that you would like to wipe the slate clean for? Now is the time to do that. Forgive yourself, forgive others. Mentally close the door on whatever it is that is not bringing light and love into your life. Make space so that when something new and positive arrives, there is somewhere for it to stay and become a part of your life.

My thoughts and feelings today:

Friday 13th December 2019

My manifesting mantra for today:

AM
9
10
11
12
1
2
3
4
5
PM

What did I learn so far this week?

Did I allow things to flow this week without trying to control the outcome?

Something I can do this weekend just for me:

My thoughts and feelings today:

Friday 13th is usually lucky for me,
may this day bring you good luck too!

Saturday 14th December 2019

My manifesting mantra for today:

AM

9

10

11

12

1

2

3

4

5

PM

What do I expect from the people closest to me?

Do I emulate the same qualities to my nearest and dearest?

Who do I need to get in touch with because it's been too long?

My thoughts and feelings today:

Sunday 15th December 2019

My manifesting mantra for today:

AM
9
10
11
12
1
2
3
4
5
PM

How have I made progress towards my life goals this week?

Three things I am grateful for:
1.
2.
3.

My thoughts and feelings today:

Monday 16th December 2019

My manifesting mantra for today:

AM

9

10

11

12

1

2

3

4

5

PM

My daily work goal to achieve this week:

What can I do today to achieve my daily work goal?

Reward if/when my daily work goal is achieved:

My thoughts and feelings today:

Tuesday 17th December 2019

My manifesting mantra for today:

AM
9
10
11
12
1
2
3
4
5
PM

As the year draws to a close, am I happy with my daily work achievements this year?

What mistakes did I make? What can I learn from this year?

What do I want to aim for next year?

My thoughts and feelings today:

Wednesday 18th December 2019

My manifesting mantra for today:

AM
9
10
11
12
1
2
3
4
5
PM

Towards the end of the year, it's a natural time to reflect back and look forward. Be willing to evaluate the results of our actions, Learn from our mistakes and make better decisions going forward. This is how we develop wisdom. How does it feel to have acted in line with our values? What effect does it have on the body and mind? Listen inwardly with a spirit of curiosity, humility and a willingness to learn. Our hearts know when our intentions are genuine and made with integrity.

My thoughts and feelings today:

Thursday 19th December 2019

My manifesting mantra for today:

AM

9

10

11

12

1

2

3

4

5

PM

What new skills would I like to develop?

What changes can I make to reduce my stress level?

Am I using my free time to do things that make me feel good?

My thoughts and feelings today:

Friday 20th December 2019

My manifesting mantra for today:

AM

9

10

11

12

1

2

3

4

5

PM

How has my energy vibration flowed this week?

What has worked well or not worked well this week?

How can I take a small step towards my best case scenario for this year?

My thoughts and feelings today:

Saturday 21st December 2019

My manifesting mantra for today:

AM
9
10
11
12
1
2
3
4
5
PM

What are my future financial needs, long term?

Am I doing enough to secure my future financial needs?

What else could I do to prepare to my future financial needs?

My thoughts and feelings today:

Sunday 22nd December 2019

My manifesting mantra for today:

AM
9
10
11
12
1
2
3
4
5
PM

Have I made progress towards or achieved my daily work goal?

If so, how? If not, why?

My favourite song at the moment and how it makes me feel:

My thoughts and feelings today:

Monday 23rd December 2019

My manifesting mantra for today:

AM

9

10

11

12

1

2

3

4

5

PM

My goal for the week ahead:

That will help me achieve my life goal of:

My priorities this week:

My thoughts and feelings today:

Tuesday 24th December 2019

My manifesting mantra for today:

AM
9
10
11
12
1
2
3
4
5
PM

How do you think the 80 year old version of yourself would remember this time in your life?

How do you want to remember this time in your life?

Make it so. If you can change something that is within your control to make your life better, do it.

My thoughts and feelings today:

"Life has no limitations, except the ones you make" - Les Brown

Wednesday 25th December 2019

My manifesting mantra for today:

AM
9
10
11
12
1
2
3
4
5
PM

Things I am grateful for this Christmas Day:

Practise connecting to your intuition: clear your mind, take three deep breaths, ask a question and trust the first thought that comes into your head. Note down the question and answer here:

Question:

Answer:

My thoughts and feelings today:

Thursday 26th December 2019

My manifesting mantra for today:

AM
9
10
11
12
1
2
3
4
5
PM

Make a wish – it's a new moon today:

What am I missing or just not seeing, right now?

What do I need to learn but won't admit to?

My thoughts and feelings today:

Friday 27th December 2019

My manifesting mantra for today:

AM

9

10

11

12

1

2

3

4

5

PM

What feelings dominated my experience of life this month?

What feelings do I want to experience in the month to come?

Am I proud of who I am, how I behave and what I offer to this world?

My thoughts and feelings today:

"You, yourself, as much as anybody in the entire Universe deserve your love and affection" - Ghandi

Saturday 28th December 2019

My manifesting mantra for today:

AM

9

10

11

12

1

2

3

4

5

PM

What have I been day dreaming about lately?

Have I spent time focusing my thoughts on positivity and what I want to happen?

Has the Universe given me any signs that it is listening?

My thoughts and feelings today:

Sunday 29th December 2019

My manifesting mantra for today:

AM
9
10
11
12
1
2
3
4
5
PM

What happened in the past month that made me feel good?

What happened in the past month that made me feel negative?

Am I living a life that is meaningful to me?

My thoughts and feelings today:

"Life is a great big canvas, and you should throw all the paint on it you can" - Danny Kaye

Monday 30th December 2019

My manifesting mantra for today:

AM
9
10
11
12
1
2
3
4
5
PM

What were my happiest moments in the past year?

How do I feel about my spiritual progress in the past year?

What area of my life should I prioritise to improve next year?

My thoughts and feelings today:

Tuesday 31st December 2019

My manifesting mantra for today:

AM

9

10

11

12

1

2

3

4

5

PM

New Year Resolutions:

My best case scenario for the year ahead:

Something that I am happy to leave behind in 2019:

My thoughts and feelings today:

"Quit hanging on to the handrails ... Let go. Surrender. Go for the ride of your life. Do it every day" - Melody Beattie

Notes

Lightning Source UK Ltd.
Milton Keynes UK
UKHW011834301118
333272UK00011B/265/P

9 781982 280185